THE
FACTS ABOUT
HINDUISM

Alison Cooper

HODDER
Wayland

an imprint of Hodder Children's Books

This book is based on the original title *Hinduism* by
Anita Ganeri, in the *What do we know about...?* series,
published in 1995 by Macdonald Young Books

This differentiated text version by Alison Cooper,
published in 2004 by Hodder Wayland, an
imprint of Hodder Children's Books
© Hodder Wayland 2004

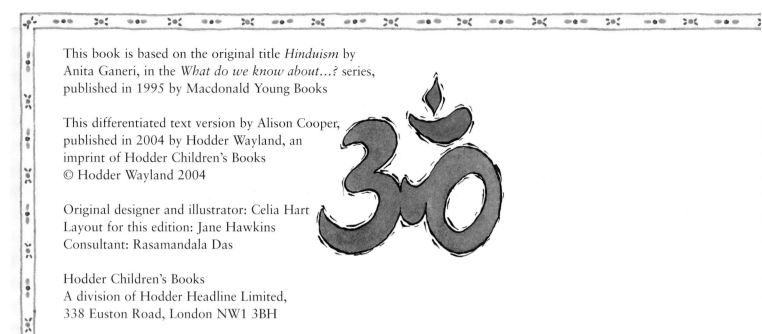

Original designer and illustrator: Celia Hart
Layout for this edition: Jane Hawkins
Consultant: Rasamandala Das

Hodder Children's Books
A division of Hodder Headline Limited,
338 Euston Road, London NW1 3BH

Photograph acknowledgements: Ancient Art & Architecture Collection, p17
(tl); The Bridgeman Art Library, London, endpapers (British Library, London)
pp38 (Freud Museum, London), 39(t) (Victoria and Albert Museum, London);
CIRCA Photo Library, pp9, 15(t), 17(b), 27(I); Dinodia/Tripp, pp21(t), 32(r),
35(c), 43; Robert Harding Picture Library, pp12(I), 20(I) (Tony Gervia), 32(I)
(JH Wilson), 35(t), 35(b) (JHC Wilson), 41(b); Michael Holford, pp13(b), 14,
16; The Hutchison Library, pp31(b), 33(r) (MacIntyre), 37; Magnum, pp15(b)
(Raghu Rai), 26 (Abbas); Bipinchandra J Mistry, p28(r); Chris Oxlade, p36(I);
Ann & Bury Peerless, pp13(t), 12(r), 18, 19(t) (br), 21(b), 22, 25(t), 27(r),
28(I), 29(t) (b), 31(c), 34, 36(r), 39(b), 42; Rex Features/Sipa-Press, p31(t);
Peter Sanders, pp23(t), 24, 25(b); Spectrum Colour Library, p40; Tony Stone
Images, pp8(I) (Anthony Cassidy), 8(r), 41(t) (David Hanson); Tripp, pp20(r)
(Helene Rogers), 23(b) (Helene Rogers), 30 (W Jacobs), 33 (I) (Helene Rogers).

Printed by WKT Company Limited

A CIP catalogue record for this book is available
from the British Library

ISBN 0 7502 46545

Endpapers: This painting shows a scene from the
Ramayana, in which Rama and Sita are living in
exile in the forest.

CONTENTS

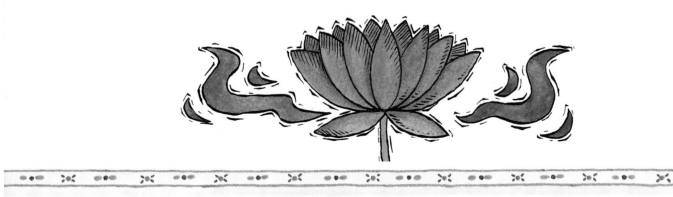

WHO ARE THE HINDUS?

Hindus are followers of a religion called Hinduism. Hinduism began in India thousands of years ago and it is one of the oldest religions in the world. Hindus themselves call their religion *sanatana dharma* which means 'eternal law' or 'eternal teaching'. Although most Hindus live in India, many have moved to other countries, such as Britain. There are also some Hindus who are not from Indian families.

◄ Holy man

This holy man is a *sannyasin* (monk) who has left home in search of God. Holy men are often called *sadhus*. They give up all their possessions and wander from place to place praying and meditating.

▲ Hindu temple

This Hindu temple is in Bali, Indonesia, showing how Hinduism has spread far from India.

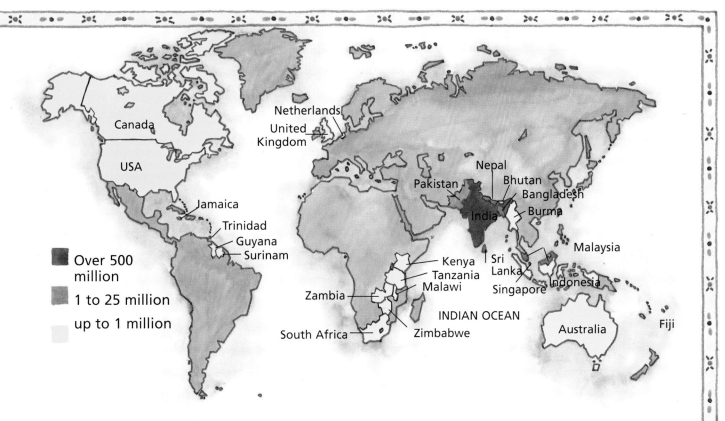

- Over 500 million
- 1 to 25 million
- up to 1 million

Canada
USA
Jamaica
Trinidad
Guyana
Surinam

Netherlands
United Kingdom

Nepal
Pakistan
Bhutan
Bangladesh
India
Burma
Malaysia
Sri Lanka
Singapore
Indonesia
Kenya
Tanzania
Malawi
Zambia
Zimbabwe
South Africa
INDIAN OCEAN
Australia
Fiji

The Hindu world

There are about 700 million Hindus worldwide. Most live in India and its nearby countries. Traders spread Hinduism to parts of Southeast Asia 1,000 years ago. Indians who went to Africa and the Caribbean in the nineteenth century took their religion with them. In the twentieth century many Hindus settled in Britain, Canada and the USA.

AN ANCIENT NAME

The word 'Hindu' was used by the ancient Persians (who lived in the area of modern-day Iran) over 2,000 years ago. They used the name to describe the people who lived east of the River Indus, in what is now Pakistan.

▲ Hindu worshippers

These worshippers are in a temple in Britain. Hindus came to Britain in the 1950s from countries such as India and Sri Lanka. Many more came from East Africa in the late 1960s and early 1970s. Today many young Hindus in Britain are British-born.

TIMELINE

CE = Common Era (this refers to the same time period as AD (Anno Domini, 'in the year of our Lord') which is traditionally used in the Christian world)
BCE = Before the Common Era

C. 3000 BCE	C. 2500 BCE	C. 1500 BCE	C 1500–1000 BCE	C. 800 BCE	C. 500 BCE
Krishna appeared and spoke to Bhagavad Gita, according to Hindu texts.	The great cities of the Indus valley are at the height of their power.	The Aryan people begin to invade India, according to scholars. Hinduism begins to develop.	The *Vedas* are used by priests. The system of 4 *varnas* and 4 *ashrams* develops.	The *Upanishads* are composed.	The Buddha spreads his teaching and lays the foundations for Buddhism.

◀ Seal used by Indus valley peoples

Buddha ▶

CE1828	CE1757	CE 1600s–1700s	CE1632	CE1570s	CE1556–1605
The Brahmo Samaj (Society of God) is founded, seeking to reform Hinduism.	India starts to come under British power and becomes part of the British Empire in 1858.	Many Europeans arrive in India, mainly to trade.	Shah Jehan builds the Taj Mahal in Agra as a memorial to his wife.	The saint Tulsi Das writes the *Ram Charit Manas*, a poem based on the *Ramayana*.	The Mogul emperor Akbar the Great is emperor of India.

CE1857
First Indian war of independence against the British.

Taj Mahal

The flag of India ▶

CE1869	CE1875	CE1876	CE1897	CE1910	CE1947
Birth of Mahatma Gandhi, a great leader in India's struggle for independence.	The Arya Samaj, another Hindu reform movement, is formed.	Queen Victoria takes the title Empress of India.	The Ramakrishna Mission is established in Calcutta.	Sri Aurobindo starts a religious centre in Pondicherry, India.	India gains independence but is split into Hindu India and Muslim Pakistan.

New countries

Britain ruled India from the late eighteenth century until 1947. Most Indians were Hindus but there were also a large number of Muslims. When India gained independence, the country's Muslims called for a separate nation to be set up where they would be free to rule themselves. Their demand was granted. The western state of Punjab and the eastern state of Bengal became West and East Pakistan. East Pakistan became Bangladesh in 1971. The partition of India led to terrible violence between Hindus and Muslims and many people were forced to leave their homes.

400BCE – CE 400 Large parts of the *Ramayana* and *Mahabharata* are composed.	CE320–550 The Gupta kings rule India – a 'golden age' for Hinduism.	C. CE700–800 The Hindu Mataram kingdom is established in Java, Indonesia.	C. CE800 The great philosopher Shankara teaches about the *Upanishads*.
			C. CE900 The Chola kings rule south India. Many beautiful temples are built.

▲ Coin of the Gupta kings

CE1526 The Muslim Mogul Empire is founded in India.	CE1469 The birth of Guru Nanak, founder of the Sikh religion. Bhakti saints popular at this time.	CE1206–1555 Muslims are powerful in the north, but a Hindu kingdom thrives in south India.	C. CE1050 Ramanuja, a Hindu philosopher, teaches devotion to a personal God, in south India.

◀ Mahatma Gandhi

Swastika ▶

CE1948 Mahatma Gandhi is assassinated.	CE 1950s–1960s Many Hindus leave India to live in Britain, Canada and the USA.	CE1960s / 1970s Many Hindus arrive in the UK, especially from East Africa, and establish the first temples.

Sign of luck ▲

In the twentieth century a version of the swastika became the symbol of the German Nazi Party. It became associated with evil. For Hindus, however, it is an ancient symbol of luck and good fortune.

HOW DID HINDUISM BEGIN?

Many Hindus believe that religion is forever and that their own tradition goes back thousands, even millions of years. Scholars say that Hinduism began over 4,000 years ago. Clay figures found in the ruins of Indus valley cities look similar to the deities (representations of God) worshipped by Hindus today.

The religion of the Indus valley people combined with the beliefs of people called the Aryans. The Aryans arrived in India from the north-west in around 1500 BCE. They worshipped many deities, mostly linked to the natural world.

Two great cities ▼

Archaeologists began excavating the Indus valley cities of Harappa and Mohenjo Daro in the 1920s. Each had a hilltop fort (see below), used as a temple and government building.

Hundreds of stone seals have been found among the ruins. Many show sacred animals such as bulls or elephants and merchants used them to mark their goods.

Seal showing a bull

▲ King or priest?

This carved stone head was found at Mohenjo Daro. It could be the head of a king, or a priest with his eyes closed in meditation.

RITUALS AND SACRIFICES

The Aryans believed that health and good harvests were dependent on the good will of God and the various deities. Their priests would throw offerings of grains, spices, butter and milk into the sacred fire. Goats and horses were sometimes sacrificed, too. As the priests performed the sacrifices, they sang hymns and chanted mantras (sacred spells). The Aryans believed that the deities could accept offerings through the flames of a fire.

Agni ▲

The carving above shows Agni, the god of fire and sacrifice. He was one of the most important Aryan deities.

◄ Indra

Indra was the most popular Aryan god, famous for his bravery and strength. He was the god of war and also of storms and thunder. His weapon was the thunderbolt. In this picture he is riding his white battle elephant.

WHAT DO HINDUS BELIEVE?

Most Hindus share the same basic beliefs, even though they do not all worship in the same way. One important teaching is reincarnation. This means that when you die your soul is reborn in the body of another human or animal. You can be reborn many times. Hindus hope that by leading a good life they will break free of the cycle of death and rebirth and achieve salvation, or *moksha*.

◀ **Sacred river**
These Hindus are bathing in the River Ganges in India. They believe that the water of the Ganges is holy. By bathing in it they wash away their sins and come closer to achieving *moksha*.

▲ **Sacred sound**
This symbol is the sound 'Om'. Hindus recite this sound during meditation and at the beginning of prayers and mantras.

◄ Monastery schools
These boys are being educated at an *ashram*. An *ashram* is a place or community for spiritual development. The boys are taught by priests and religious teachers called *gurus*. The pupils treat their *gurus* with great respect. Adult Hindus sometimes spend time at an *ashram* to seek spiritual guidance.

A way of life ▶
Hindus try to follow a sacred code of behaviour called *dharma*. This means serving God and doing their duty to family, friends and society. Religion affects everything in their daily life from working honestly to the food they eat, which is often vegetarian.

 PATHS TO FOLLOW

There are four paths Hindus can follow to reach *moksha*.

- The Path of Devotion – prayer, worship and devotion to God.
- The Path of Knowledge – study and learning, with a guru's guidance.
- The Path of Right Action – acting without any thought of reward for yourself.
- The Path of Yoga – yoga and meditation.

WHICH ARE THE MAIN HINDU DEITIES?

The deities of Hinduism represent different characteristics of Brahman, the supreme soul or spirit. Brahman is all around, in everything, all the time. The

three main deities are Brahma the creator, Vishnu the protector, and Shiva the destroyer.

A Hindu may worship more than one deity, though they often have a favourite or one they consider to be the supreme deity (God). Often, a family has worshipped certain deities for several generations.

◄ Brahma

This is a statue of Brahma, the creator of the universe and the god of wisdom. The sacred statue has four faces (although only three can be seen in this photograph). This shows that Brahma looks over the whole world – north, south, east and west. He has four arms too, in which he holds the sacred books, the prayer beads and the water pot of a holy man. Brahma, although important as the creator, is only worshipped in one place in India.

Shiva ▼

Shiva, the destroyer of the world, is often shown dancing. The dance represents the energy flowing through the world, which causes day and night, the changing seasons, death and rebirth.

Dancing Shiva

Vishnu ▲

The painting above shows Vishnu, the protector of the universe, with his wife, Lakshmi. She is the goddess of wealth and good fortune. Vishnu has come to earth nine times, in nine different forms, or *avatars*, to save the world. These include Lord Rama, Lord Krishna and Buddha. The tenth *avatar* of Vishnu is Kalki, the rider on the white horse, who is yet to come.

RIDING ANIMALS

The various deities ride on different animals. For example, Brahma rides on a swan, Vishnu rides on a giant eagle (above) and Shiva rides on a white bull called Nandi (right).

DO HINDUS WORSHIP OTHER DEITIES?

There are thousands of Hindu deities. Some are worshipped all over India, others are honoured in just one or two villages. The most worshipped are Vishnu, Shiva and the goddess Parvati.

Rama and Krishna are two of the *avatars* (forms) of Vishnu. Parvati is the wife of Shiva. Like many Hindu deities, she has other names, representing her different aspects. When she is worshipped as Kali or Durga, she is awesome and terrifying. She represents the destruction of evil and the protection of good.

◀ Rama and Sita

The picture on the left shows Rama, his wife Sita and his faithful friend, Hanuman, the monkey god. The story of Rama and Sita is told in the great poem the *Ramayana* (see pages 42-43). Rama is worshipped as an ideal human being – a great hero, a devoted husband and a just king.

SUN AND MOON

Surya, the sun god, rides across the sky each morning in his golden chariot. His wife, Ushas, is goddess of the dawn.

Surya

The silver chariot of Chandra, the moon god, crosses the sky as darkness falls.

Chandra

◀ Krishna

Krishna is usually shown with dark blue or black skin and carrying or playing a flute. He is often surrounded by cows and milkmaids, too. Krishna is famous for playing tricks on his friends and is the hero of many adventures.

Durga ▶

Durga is the warlike form of the goddess Parvati. In this picture she is riding on a fierce tiger and holding a different weapon in each of her ten hands.

Ganesha ▲

Ganesha is the son of Shiva and Parvati. Hindus pray to him before they begin anything new because he is the god who removes obstacles.

HOW DO HINDU FAMILIES LIVE?

It is traditional for Hindus to share their home with their parents, grandparents, uncles, aunts and cousins. Large family groups like this are known as joint or extended families. Children learn about their religion from their parents and grandparents. They are taught to respect the older members of their family.

◄ **Family names**

Hindus rarely call one another by their first names. They use special titles that describe how they are related. For example, you would call your father's younger brother *chachaji* and his wife *chachiji*. The man in the centre of the photograph on the left has just married the girl in the red sari. She will soon be getting to know his relatives because she will live in their family home.

Caste system ►

Hindus divided society into four groups called *varnas*. Traditionally, this was based on the jobs people did. The highest *varna* is the priests. Next come the warriors and nobles, and after them the merchants. Below them are the labourers, like the potters in this photograph. The present system, based on the community you are born in, is called the caste system.

Sweets

Vegetarian food ▲

Many Hindus are vegetarians because they think it is wrong to kill animals to eat. A typical meal might include a spicy vegetable dish, rice, dahl and flat bread. With their meal people drink water, sweet tea or a yoghurt drink called *lassi*.

◀ **Indian sweets** ▲

Many Hindus love sweets and they are often given as gifts at weddings and festivals. Milk, cheese, nuts, coconut and sugar are popular ingredients.

Sacred cows ▲

Hindus believe that the cow is very special because she is a mother that produces milk, a precious source of food. Wherever you go in India you will see cows wandering freely, even in the towns.

NAMES

Many Hindu children are named after deities, or have names that are linked to their religion.

Boys
Rajendra – Lord Indra
Mahesh – a name of Shiva

Girls
Devi – goddess
Vandana – worshipper

WHERE DO HINDUS WORSHIP?

For many Hindus there are no set rules about where they should worship, or when. Some Hindus set up a shrine in a room at home and worship there. They also worship in buildings called temples, or *mandirs*. Some people visit the temple every day. Others only go there at special times, such as festivals. Hindu temples are often noisy, lively places, filled with the sound of praying, chanting and singing.

◄ **Temples**

This is the entrance gateway of a temple in southern India. It is decorated with carvings of the deity. People think of the temple as the earthly home of God. This temple is dedicated to Shiva.

Temple bell ▲

As worshippers enter the temple, they ring the bell to announce their arrival.

Street shrines ▶

On many street corners there are small shrines like this one, where Hindus can stop to worship on their way to work or school. They might leave an offering of flowers or sweets for the deity. This shrine is dedicated to Shiva. You can see the white bull Nandi in the bottom left corner.

 MORE TEMPLES

The only temple in India dedicated to Brahma is in Pushkar, in western India. In southern India, at Mahabalipuram, there is a group of very beautiful stone temples. They are 1,400 years old. The town is still famous for the skill of its sculptors.

Temples at Mahabalipuram

◀ Worship at home

The photograph on the left shows a shrine in a Hindu home. It is dedicated to Saraswati, the goddess of art and music and the wife of Brahma. The brass pots on the floor contain leaves, flowers and sweets, which the family will offer to the goddess for her blessing.

HOW DO HINDUS WORSHIP?

There is no set time when Hindus should visit the temple – but mornings and evenings are most important. Before they enter the building, they take off their shoes. Women often cover their heads, to show respect. Hindus go to the temple to take *darshan* of the deity as well as for group worship. *Darshan* means a 'seeing' of the image or statue in the inner sanctum that shows the presence of the deity.

▲ The inner sanctum

A priest sits near the image of the deity in the inner sanctum, the holiest part of the temple. Only the priest is allowed to get so close to the sacred image.

◀ Temple offerings

Outside the temple, worshippers can buy offerings of flowers, fruit, incense and coloured powder at stalls like this one. They give their offerings to the priest and he presents them to the temple deity to be blessed. Then he hands them back to the worshipper, to carry the deity's blessing back to them. This ceremony is part of *puja*.

In the temple ▶

These worshippers are waiting for a *darshana* (sight) of the god Hanuman. They are holding offerings of flower garlands and small lamps. As part of their worship they circle the shrine. They always walk in a clockwise direction to keep their right sides facing towards the god and the inner sanctum.

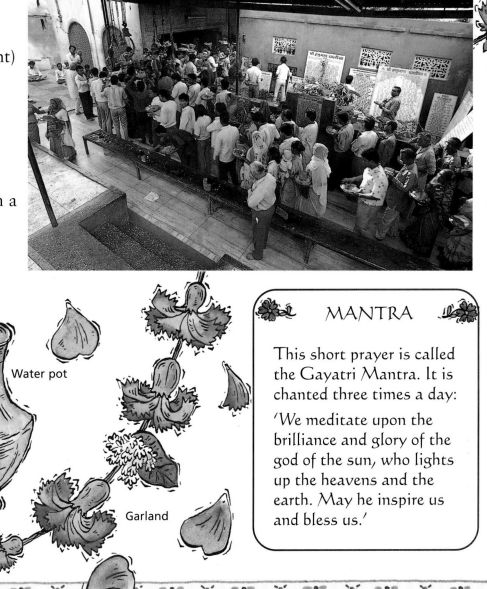

Water pot

Garland

MANTRA

This short prayer is called the Gayatri Mantra. It is chanted three times a day:

'We meditate upon the brilliance and glory of the god of the sun, who lights up the heavens and the earth. May he inspire us and bless us.'

WHO ARE HINDU HOLY MEN?

Hindu holy men include priests, *gurus* and *sannyasins*. A *sannyasin* is a person who has given up his home, family and posessions to lead a life of prayer and meditation. Some holy men wander from place to place and rely on local people to give them food and shelter. Others live on an *ashram* and learn from a *guru*, or teacher.

Holy man ▶

This holy man, or *sadhu*, is a follower of Shiva. The cloth he is wearing around his waist is of a colour called saffron, which is a holy colour. He is meditating on the banks of the River Ganges. Many Hindus worship not only God but also holy men, especially *gurus*, and dedicate shrines to them.

HOLY WORDS

These are some words spoken by famous Hindu holy men:

'I have nothing new to teach the world. Truth and non-violence are as old as the hills.'
  Mahatma Gandhi

'A person who accepts a gift from the gods and does not repay it is a thief.'
  Sri Aurobindo

Ramakrishna ▼

A holy man called Ramakrishna taught that all religions were equal. He believed in Jesus Christ and in Muhammad, the founder of Islam, as well as in the Hindu gods. This temple belongs to the Ramakrishna Mission, which spread Ramakrishna's message.

Yoga and meditation ▼

Many Hindus use yoga exercises and meditation. They train their bodies and minds to achieve *moksha*. Some people concentrate hard on a pattern to help them focus their minds. These patterns are called *yantras*.

Priests ▲

Every temple has its own priest *(pujari)*, who looks after the image of the temple deity and performs the *puja* (ritual worship). Most Hindus have their own family priest, who comes to their home to carry out important ceremonies.

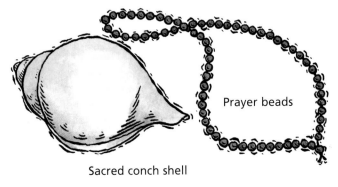

Prayer beads

Sacred conch shell

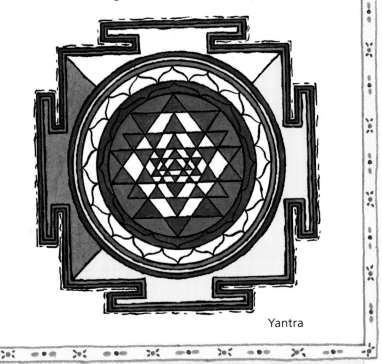

Yantra

WHICH ARE THE HINDUS' SACRED BOOKS?

The *Vedas* are the oldest of the Hindus' sacred books. They date from the time of the Aryans and are over 3,000 years old. Another important collection of teachings is the *Upanishads*. Hindus believe that a group of wise men heard the words of the *Upanishads* and the *Vedas* directly from God.

The *Mahabharata* and the *Ramayana* are two long poems. These were also made up long ago and people learned them by heart. The words were passed down from one generation to another.

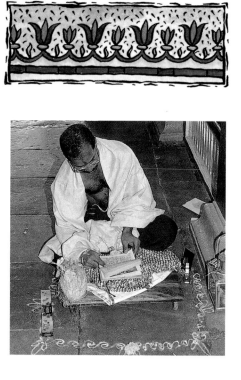

The *Upanishads* ▶

The photograph on the right shows words from the *Upanishads* carved on the wall of a temple in Varanasi, India. The *Upanishads* focus on the relationship between the *atman* (soul) and Brahman (the Supreme). These sacred teachings date from around 800 BCE.

श्रीलक्ष्मीनारायण

एक ही ईश्वर के अनेक नाम
स ब्रह्मा स शिवः सेन्द्रः सोऽक्षरः परमः स्वराट् ।
स एव विष्णुः स प्राणः स कालोऽग्निः स चन्द्रमाः॥ (केवल्य उप. १/८)
सर्वशक्तिमान् और समस्त जगत् का प्रकाशक वह परमात्मा ही ब्रह्मा (सृष्टि-कर्ता) है वही शिव रुद्र
(विनाशक शक्ति) है, वही विष्णु (पालन करने वाली शक्ति) है वही इन्द्र है अविनाशी है वही सर्वव्यापक
है, वही जगत् का जीवनाधार है वही काल है, अग्नि है, और चन्द्रमा है।
He is one and only one God
THAT ALMIGHTY, ALLPERVADING GOD IS BRAHMA, THE CREATIVE FORM,
VISHNU THE PROTECTIVE FORM AND SHIVA, THE DESTRUCTIVE FORM. HE IS
INDRA; HE IS IMMORTAL; HE IS SELF-EXISTENT AND SELF-EFFULGENT.
HE IS LIFE-FORM, HE IS TIME, HE IS FIRE AND HE IS MOON. (K.UPANISHAD 1/8)

◀ *Bhagavad Gita*

The *Bhagavad Gita* is the most important and popular part of the *Mahabharata*. The *Mahabharata* tells the story of a war between two royal families, the Kauravas and the Pandavas, who are cousins. They both want to control the kingdom of Hastinapura, but the Pandavas are its rightful rulers.

The *Bhagavad Gita*, the 'Song of the Lord', is set on the battlefield. The painting shows Arjuna, one of the Pandavas, in his chariot. Lord Krishna is his charioteer. Arjuna tells Krishna how sad he feels because he is about to fight his cousins. Krishna tells him to control his emotions and do his duty as a warrior. Acting selflessly is the way to achieve *moksha*. Arjuna follows Krishna's advice and eventually the Kaurava army is destroyed.

SANSKRIT

Sanskrit is the ancient language of the Aryans. It is the language that was used when the *Vedas* and the *Upanishads* were written down. Sanskrit is not much spoken now although it is still studied by priests. Hindi, the modern language of India, developed from it.

◀ The *Ramayana*

The *Ramayana* tells the story of Rama and Sita (you can read the story on pages 42–43). The poem was made up over 2,000 years ago but the most famous version was written in the 1570s by Tulsi Das, who is shown in the picture on the left. It has also been made into a television series.

WHICH ARE THE HINDUS' SACRED PLACES?

Many sacred places are connected to events in the lives of various deities and the many Hindu saints. Some are famous for their beauty or because people have been miraculously healed there. Every year millions of Hindus set off on journeys to visit sacred places. These journeys are called pilgrimages. People might go on a pilgrimage to ask God or specific deities to grant them a special request, or to give thanks to them. Sometimes people walk for many days to reach a place of pilgrimage.

◀ Holy places

This map shows some of the holiest places in India. Hindus believe they can pass beyond this world to obtain *moksha* at some of these sites.

Varanasi ▶

The city of Varanasi is the holiest place of pilgrimage. Hindu legends say that Shiva chose Varanasi as his home on earth. Most Hindus believe Varanasi is the best place to die and many go there to scatter the ashes of their dead relatives in the River Ganges. Pilgrims wash away their sins in its holy waters.

◀ Bathing fairs

◀ Bathing fairs

Every twelve years, a great fair is held at Allahabad. Over two million pilgrims come to bathe at the point where the River Ganges, the River Yamuna and the mythical River Saraswati flow together. This type of fair is called a *kumbha mela*.

LEGEND OF THE GANGES

There was once a king who begged Shiva to let the magical River Ganges fall to earth. Shiva agreed to his request, but to make sure the earth would not shatter under the weight of the water, he caught the river in his hair. Then he let it flow down gently from the Himalayas.

Rameshwaram ▲

This is the Ramanathaswamy temple on the island of Rameshwaram in south India. Rama is said to have worshipped here after his battle with Ravana (see pages 42–43). It is an important place of pilgrimage.

Sacred mountains ▶

The Himalayan mountains that stretch across northern India are the highest mountains in the world. Many of them are holy places. These pilgrims are making the difficult journey to Gangotri, the source of the River Ganges.

WHAT ARE THE MAIN HINDU FESTIVALS?

Hindus hold festivals to celebrate important events in the lives of their deities and saints. Festivals are also linked to the changing seasons and to harvest time. There are far too many festivals for everyone to celebrate all of them but most Hindus celebrate Diwali, Holi and Dussehra. For Hindus living outside India, festivals are an important way for children to learn about their religion and a time for families and friends to get together.

◀ Local festivals

These women are preparing offerings. Local festivals celebrate the harvest or honour the village deities. Some festivals, such as the kite-flying festival in western India, are not religious – they are just good fun.

Kite

Diwali ▶

Diwali is the Hindu festival of lights and it is celebrated in late October or early November. People light small oil lamps and place them by their doors and windows to guide Rama back home (see the story on pages 42–43). They enjoy firework displays and delicious food. They also give each other cards and presents.

Dussehra ▶

The Dussehra festival is held in October. For most Hindus it is a celebration of Rama's victory over the demon king, Ravana. Giant models of Ravana are used in a performance of the story.

Holi ▲

Holi is the liveliest and messiest festival of the year. It is held in March to celebrate the coming of spring. People put on old clothes and pelt each other with coloured water and powder. After a bath and change of clothes they visit their relatives to wish them happy Holi.

Raksha Bandhan ▶

At Raksha Bandhan brothers and sisters show their affection for each other. Girls tie bracelets called *rakhis* around their brothers' wrists. Boys give their sisters a gift.

Rakhi bracelets

HINDU CALENDAR

HINDU MONTH	
Chaitra	March–April
Vaisakha	April–May
Jyaishtha	May–June
Ashadha	June–July
Shravana	July–August
Bhadra	August–September
Ashvina	September–October
Karttika	October–November
Margashirsha	November–December
Pausha	December–January
Magha	January–February
Phalguna	February–March

WHAT ARE THE MOST IMPORTANT TIMES IN A HINDU'S LIFE?

Hindus mark important times in their lives with ceremonies called *samskaras*. These begin even before a baby is born, with prayers for it to be healthy and happy. Once the baby arrives there are ceremonies to mark its birth, the first time it sees the sun and its first haircut.

Getting married is another important occasion marked with a *samskara*. The final ceremonies take place when a person dies and is cremated.

Horoscope ▶

The picture on the right is a horoscope for a baby boy. It shows the position of the stars and planets at the exact moment of the baby's birth. A priest draws up the horoscope and uses it to work out what may happen to the baby in the future. This is done at the baby's naming ceremony, which usually takes place ten days after its birth.

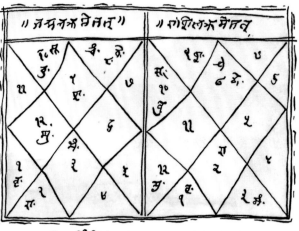

Baby boy's horoscope

▼ Sacred thread

Boys from the top three *varnas* – Brahmins, Kshatriyas and Vaishyas – go through the sacred thread ceremony when they are about nine or ten years old. A priest loops a cotton thread over the boy's left shoulder and under his right arm. This marks the start of his adult life. He can now begin to study the holy books and take more responsibility within the family.

◀ A Hindu wedding ▼

A Hindu wedding lasts for several days and often 15 rituals are performed. In the photograph on the left the bride and groom are exchanging flower garlands. The bride below is wearing beautiful jewellery. The groom will give her a special necklace.

STAGES OF LIFE

A Hindu man's life is traditionally divided into four stages (ashrams):
Brahmachari – Life as a student
Grihastha – Married life
Vanaprastha – Retirement
Sannyas – Life as a wandering holy man

Death and cremation ▶

Hindus are almost always cremated. The person's eldest son or male relation lights the fire while a priest chants from the holy books. Burning the body helps the soul give up attachment to the body and move onto the next life. If possible, people scatter the ashes of their dead relative in the River Ganges.

WHAT IS TRADITIONAL HINDU MEDICINE?

Traditional Hindu medicine is called Ayurveda, which means the 'science of long life'. Ayurvedic medicine has changed very little in thousands of years.

Ayurvedic doctors are called *vaidyas*. They believe that the body contains three 'humours' – bile, wind and mucus. When people become ill, it is because they have too much or too little of one of these humours. The *vaidya's* treatment brings the humours back into balance again. Eating healthy foods, taking exercise and doing yoga are also important ways of keeping the body's humours balanced.

Sacred herb ▼

The girl below is looking after a tulsi bush. Tulsi is a herb and it is believed to be very good for healing. People think of it as a sacred plant, linked to Vishnu. They often plant tulsi bushes to bring them good luck.

▲ Ayurvedic chemist's shop

This chemist's shop in western India is run by the government. It sells Ayurvedic medicines. Many people prefer Ayurvedic medicines to modern drugs, although some use a mixture of the two. There are hundreds of different ingredients in Ayurvedic medicines, including plants, herbs, spices and oils.

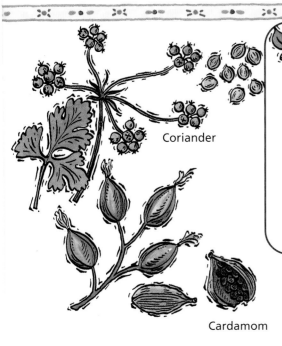
Coriander

Cardamom

NATURAL MEDICINES

The herbs and spices shown on this page are all used to treat different health problems.

Coriander – good for the digestion and skin problems
Cardamom – good for the heart and lungs
Black pepper – good for treating loss of appetite and to reduce swelling
Ginger – good for headaches, sore throats and colds

Pepper

Ginger

Healthy living

Here is a suggested Ayurvedic routine for a healthy life.

- Wake up early, before sunrise.
- Go to the toilet regularly.
- Have a bath every morning.
- Eat breakfast before 8 a.m.
- Wash your hands before and after eating.
- Eat slowly and in silence.
- Take a short walk 15 minutes after a meal.
- Go to sleep before 10 p.m.

Street seller ▶

This street seller has spread out dried plants, roots and herbs on the pavement. The metal bar in front of him is his weighing scale.

WHAT IS HINDU ART LIKE?

A lot of Hindu art is linked to religion. There are many sacred statues of the deities. Often these are made for the inner sanctum of the temple or a family shrine. They are a symbol of God's presence on earth. Hindu artists also produce beautiful paintings and carvings that show scenes and stories from the sacred books. Many of the tools used by artists and sculptors have not changed in hundreds of years.

◀ Sacred statue of Vishnu

This statue of Vishnu is carved from ivory. It shows him sitting on the coils of a serpent while he waits for Brahma to create the world. In his four arms he holds the signs of his divinity and power: a conch shell, a lotus flower, a club and a discus (spinning disc used as a weapon).

Symbol of Shiva ▼

The picture below shows a *lingam*, carved in stone or marble. It is a symbol of Shiva's presence and power. In temples dedicated to Shiva there is often a *lingam* in the inner sanctum instead of a sacred statue of the god.

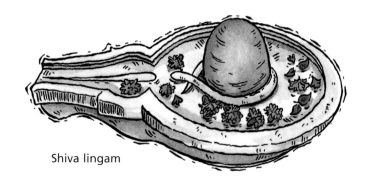

Shiva lingam

Hindu painting ▶

Artists in Rajasthan, western India, painted this picture in the 1700s. It shows Vishnu surrounded by his ten *avatars* (see page 17). From left to right they are: (top row) Matsysa the fish, Kurma the tortoise, Varaha the boar; (second row) Narasimha the man-lion, Vamana the dwarf; (third row) Parashurama the warrior, Rama; (bottom row) Krishna, the Buddha and Kalki, the horseman.

A modern temple ▼

The temple below was built in Varanasi in 1964 in honour of the poet Tulsi Das. In the 1570s he produced a very famous version of the *Ramayana* called the *Ram Charit Manas*.

SYMBOLS USED IN ART

The swastika is an ancient sign of good fortune.

Om stands for perfection.

The lotus flower is a symbol of Vishnu.

The *Shri* symbol is a sign of wellbeing.

DO HINDUS LIKE MUSIC AND DANCE?

Hindus love music and dance, and there are many different kinds. Classical Hindu music and dance follow strict rules, which were invented thousands of years ago. Religious hymns called *bhajans* are sung in temples. Stories from the *Mahabharata* and the *Ramayana* are set to music or performed in dance. Each region of India has its own folk dances and songs, which are performed at festival times.

Tanpura

Shahnai

Rudra-vina

▲ Classical music

Indian classical music is based on one of several melodies, called *ragas*. Each *raga* has a different mood, such as joy or sadness. The musicians are playing (left to right) *tablas* (drums), a *sitar* (played like a guitar) and a *sarangi* (played with a bow, like a cello).

MUSICAL INSTRUMENTS

The pictures above right show:

Tanpura – a stringed instrument over one metre long.

Shahnai – a wind instrument like an oboe, with seven holes.

Rudra-vina – a stringed instrument with two 'bowls'.

◄ Make-up

The Kathakali dancer on the left is putting on his make-up. The costume and make-up of each dancer show what type of character he is. Green means good, red means brave or fierce, black means evil and white means pure.

Vishnu

Hand signals ►

It takes many years of training to become a classical dancer. Each movement of the eyes, head and hands has a special meaning, and there are hundreds of movements to learn.

Shiva

Kathakali dancers ▼

The masked dancers below are performing a Kathakali dance. This style of dancing is from southern India. All the dancers are men and they perform very dramatic dances based on the great Hindu poems.

Birds

Peacock

Beautiful

Sorrowful

DO HINDUS LIKE STORIES?

Hindus have enjoyed stories for thousands of years. Before the sacred books were written down, storytellers learned them by heart and went

from village to village, telling tales of the deities and heroes such as Rama and Krishna. Hindu children still read these stories in comic books and watch them on television. One of the best-loved tales is this story of Rama and Sita.

The story of the *Ramayana*

Rama was the eldest son of the king of Ayodhya, a city in northern India. Rama was the rightful heir to the throne but his stepmother wanted her own son, Bharata, to be the king's heir. She persuaded the king to banish Rama from the kingdom for fourteen years. Sadly, Rama left home with his wife, Sita, and his brother, Lakshman, and they went to live in the forest.

One day, while Rama and Lakshman were out hunting deer, Sita was kidnapped by Ravana, the demon king of Lanka. Rama and Lakshman looked for her everywhere but she had vanished without trace. Eventually Rama asked his friend Hanuman, the monkey god,

to help. Hanuman was the leader of a great army and had many magical powers.

After searching for a long time, Hanuman discovered that Ravana had taken Sita to Lanka, his island across the sea. With a giant leap he soared over the sea to the island and found Sita in the palace garden, surrounded by demon guards. But before Hanuman could get away to tell Rama, the guards caught him. Ravana tied him up with ropes and ordered the guards to set fire to his tail. Sita prayed to the gods to save Hanuman and they did. He escaped with only a singed tail.

Rama and Lakshman gathered a huge army, led by Hanuman and Jambhavan, the king of the bears. They built a bridge across the sea to Lanka and marched across it to do battle. Ravana sent his most terrifying demons to fight them and the battle raged all night. In the morning, Rama and Lakshman lay bleeding among the wounded.

Quickly, Hanuman realised what he must do. He dashed away to bring healing herbs from the top of a mountain and with them saved his friends' lives. Now it was time for Rama to face the demon king himself.

Ravana ▲

The ten-headed demon king ruled the island that is now called Sri Lanka. He had been told that if he married Sita he would become ruler of the world.

Ravana raced towards Rama in his war chariot. Calmly, Rama fitted a golden arrow to his golden bow and fired it at Ravana's heart. With a dreadful shriek Ravana fell from his chariot and died.

At last Rama and Sita were reunited. Together with Lakshman and Hanuman they returned to Ayodhya. There, they were crowned king and queen and everyone rejoiced to see them.

••••

The story of Rama and Sita is acted out during the festival of Dussehra (see page 33).

▲ **Play acting**
These children are dressed as Rama and Sita.

43

GLOSSARY

Aryans The people who invaded India from the north-west in around 1500 BCE. Their religious beliefs formed the beginnings of Hinduism.

avatar A god or goddess in human or animal form.

conch shell A large shell that makes a sound when you blow into it. When Vishnu blows into the conch shell he is calling on humankind to turn away from evil.

cremation The burning of a dead body until only ashes remain.

deity A god or goddess.

demon An evil spirit.

inner sanctum The holiest part of the temple, where an image of the god or goddess is kept in a shrine.

lotus flower Hindu deities are often shown holding or standing on a lotus flower. It is a sign of purity and beauty.

meditation Sitting quietly and focusing on a word or picture until you become totally calm and peaceful.

moksha The freedom of the soul from the cycle of death and rebirth. A Hindu's aim is to achieve *moksha*.

Muslim A follower of Islam, the religion founded by the Prophet Muhammad in CE 610.

prayer beads Beads that a worshipper uses to help him or her to concentrate on a series of prayers – they count a bead as they say each prayer.

sacred Holy; devoted to a god or goddess; or used for a religious purpose.

sacrifice To offer something to the deities. Making a sacrifice might involve killing a person or animal to please the deities.

salvation To be saved; for Hindus it means to be released from the cycle of death and rebirth (*moksha*).

shrine A place where images of the gods are kept and honoured. This might be in the home or in a temple.

temple The building where Hindus worship; it is also known as a *mandir*.

varna One of four groups into which Hindu society was organised. Originally a person's varna was decided by the job they did. People are now born into a particular varna and are often expected to marry someone from the same caste (community).

yoga Physical and mental exercises that people carry out to become completely calm and clear in their thoughts.

INDEX